THE REALITY OF NEW BIRTH

*Jesus answered, Verily, verily, I say unto thee,
Except a man be born of water and of the Spirit,
he cannot enter into the kingdom of God.*
John 3:15

by
Franklin N. Abazie

The Reality of New Birth
COPYRIGHT @ 2016 by Franklin N. Abazie
ISBN: 978-1-94513317-6

All right reserved. This book or any portion thereof may not be reproduced or used in any manner whatsoever without the express written permission of the publisher, except for the use of brief quotations in a book review. All Bible quotes are from King James Version and others as noted.

Published by: F N ABAZIE PUBLISHING HOUSE—
a.k.a. Empowerment Bookstore

*That I may publish with the voice of thanksgiving
and tell of all thy wondrous works.*
Psalms 26:7

To order additional copies, wholesales or booking call:
the Church office (973.372.7518)
or Empowerment Bookstore Hotline (973.393.8518)

Worship address:
343 Sanford Avenue, Newark, New Jersey 07106
Administrative Head Office address:
33 Schley Street Newark New Jersey 07112
Email: pastorfranknto@yahoo.com
Website www.fnabaziehealingministries.org
Publishing House: www.fnabaziepublishinghouse.org

This book is a production of F N Abazie Publishing House. A publication Arms of Miracle of God Ministries 2016.
First Edition

CONTENTS

THE MANDATE OF THE COMMISSION....................iv
ARMS OF THE COMMISSION...................................v
INTRODUCTION..vi

CHAPTER 1
Walking in the Newness of Life..................................1

CHAPTER 2
Understanding the New Annointing.......................20

CHAPTER 3
The Benefit of the New Annointing........................24

CHAPTER 4
Walking in the Reality of New Birth........................31

CHAPTER 5
Prayer of Salvation...53
ABOUT THE AUTHOR...60
OTHER BOOKS BY THE AUTHOR.............................61

THE MANDATE OF THE COMMISSION

"The moment is due to impact your world through the revival of the healing & miracle ministry of Jesus Christ of Nazareth.

"I am sending you to restore health unto thee and I will heal thee of thy wounds, said the Lord of Host."

ARMS OF THE COMMISSION

1) F N Abazie Ministries—Miracle of God Ministries (Miracle Chapel Intl)

2) F N Abazie TV Ministries: Global Television Ministry Outreach

3) F N Abazie Radio Ministries: Radio Broadcasting Outreach

4) F N Abazie Publishing House: Book Publication

5) F N Abazie Bible School: also called Word of Healing Bible School (W.O.H.B.S.)

6) F N Abazie Evangelistic Ass: Miracle of God Ministries: Global Crusade

7) Empowerment Bookstore: Book distribution

8) F N Abazie Helping Hands: Meeting the Help of the Needy Worldwide

9) F N Abazie Disaster Recovery Mission: Global Disaster Recovery

10) F N Abazie Prison Ministry: Prison Ministry For All Convicts "Second Chance"

Some of our ministry arms are awaiting the appointed time to commence.

INTRODUCTION

Just one outstanding scripture summarizes my introduction of this book: ***THE REALITY OF NEW BIRTH.***

Jesus answered and said unto him, *"Verily, verily, I say unto thee, Except a man be born again, he cannot see the kingdom of God."* (John 3:3) That is my introduction in a nutshell.

Jesus answered, Verily, verily, I say unto thee,
Except a man be born of water and of the Spirit,
he cannot enter into the kingdom of God.
John 3:5

Do not be IGNORANT. We live in a desperate time, where immoralities—the pleasure of sin—have overtaken our hearts. Many people do not even believe in God, nor agree with new birth—of being BORN AGAIN. It was Nicodemus, the Ruler of the Jews, who posed this outstanding question to Jesus.

Nicodemus saith unto him, How can a man be born
when he is old? can he enter the second time into his
mother's womb, and be born?
John 3:4

Acknowledge therefore that it takes the conviction of the HOLY SPIRIT to convince and convict anyone to accept JESUS CHRIST. Unless the HOLY SPIRIT brings CONVICTION, no matter how much grammar I use in this book, it will still not make sense to you. THE HOLY SPIRIT is an advocate and a representative of the supreme sovereign power of God. As a messenger, He is supervising all we do, including accepting JESUS as our LORD and personal SAVIOR. *For in Him we live, and move, and have our being; as certain also of your own poets have said, For we are also his offspring.* (Acts 17:20)

For it is God who is working in you, enabling you both to desire and to work out His good purpose.
Philippians 2:13

There is nothing we—believers and non-believers—can achieve and innovate in this race of life without the help of the Holy Spirit. Consider that in the New Testament, the Holy Spirit is the Spirit of CONVICTION and JUDGEMENT (see John 16:8-11).

THE HOLY SPIRIT IS THE SPIRIT OF CONVICTION & JUDGEMENT

And when He is come, He will reprove the world of sin, and of righteousness, and of judgment: Of sin, because they believe not on me; Of righteousness, because I go to my Father, and ye see me no more; Of judgment, because the prince of this world is judged.
John 16:8-11

It is impossible for my writing to CONVINCE and CONVICT anyone of new birth. **THE REALITY OF NEW BIRTH**, in my own interpretation, means there is something BIGGER SPIRITUALLY than just being "BORN AGAIN." As believers we must experience GOD in a supernatural way. We are not supposed to struggle to accomplish anything in life. We must not go through depression, difficulties and challenges in life. God MUST establish and arrange everything in life for us in a SUPER WAY for us as believers.

Contrary to the known norm, BORN AGAIN CHRISTIAN does not mean we must be "poor people." To be rich or poor is a choice we make in life. So many of us missed it. That you are a BORN AGAIN believer who speaks in tongue and worships every Sunday does not exempt you from the challenges of life. *These things I have spoken unto you, that in me ye might have peace. In the world ye shall have tribulation: but be of good cheer; I have overcome the world.* (John 16:33)

Come with me as we unfold **THE REALITY OF NEW BIRTH**.

HAPPY READING!

PRAYER POINT TO ACTIVATE THE PRESENCE OF THE HOLY SPIRIT

1) Holy Spirit, reveal yourself to me, in the Name of Jesus.

2) Holy Spirit, crush every daily habit of sin, in the Name of Jesus.

3) Holy Spirit, become my companion today, in the Name of Jesus.

4) Holy Spirit, grant me access, in the Name of Jesus.

5) Power of God, grant me the GRACE to live right for Jesus Christ.

6) Hand of God, deliver me from sin, in the Name of Jesus.

7) Fire of God, burn every sinful thoughts from my mind, in the Name of Jesus.

I proclaim authority over
every prevailing sin in my life, in Jesus Name.

8) I destroy every root of sin in my life, in Jesus Name.

9) Sin shall not have dominion over my life, in the Name of Jesus.

10) Lord God, emphasize genuine repentance over my spirit man, in the Name of Jesus

11) Holy Spirit, revive and rekindle your fire of revival inside of me, in the Name of Jesus.

12) Power of God, hijack the controlling forces oppressing my life, in the Name of Jesus.

13) Blood of Jesus, take over my life, in the Name of Jesus.

14) O Lord, baptize me with the gift of the Holy Spirit.

15) Holy Spirit, breathe afresh upon my life, in the Name of Jesus.

16) Holy Spirit, take possession of my will, in the Name of Jesus.

17) Holy Spirit, make yourself real to me, in the name of Jesus.

Holy Spirit, fan your revival fire upon my life, in the name of Jesus.

CONGRATULATIONS!

AS a Born Again Christian, we must all experience THE REALITY OF NEW BIRTH.

I give special thanks to GOD for your life.

If you have not received the Lord Jesus Christ as your personal savior, repeat after me and say—

Lord Jesus,
I accept you today, as my Lord, and as my savior.
Forgive me of my sins, wash me with your blood,
right now. I believe, I am santified, I am free, I am saved.
I am free from the power of sin, to serve the Lord Jesus.
Thank you, Lord for saving me.
Amen.

CHAPTER 1
WALKING IN THE NEWNESS OF LIFE

*Therefore if any man be in Christ,
he is a new creature: old things are passed away;
behold, all things are become new.*
2 Corinthians 5:17

Most new Christian converts do not know this truth—new birth is the foundation for the new anointing. So many Christians profess and confess to being born again by the Spirit of God. The question is: ***Are you TRULY Born Again?***

The scripture above says if any man be in Christ, he is a new creature. When we are truly born again, even the birds in the air know it. The devil fears genuine BORN AGAIN BELIEVERS. The **REAL Born Again Believers are supposed to be in command and in authority over every affair of their lives**.

There is so much confusion in the body of CHRIST here in AMERICA and in NIGERIA that we truly cannot differentiate ourselves from non-believers and from those of the other faith (Muslims). There must be significant difference among us that follow the LORD JESUS CHRIST.

Be ye followers of me, even as I also am of Christ.
1 Corninthians 1:11

We cannot follow the Lord JESUS CHRIST and not experience the anointing upon him.

As a believer, there must be some unique difference between us all. When we became Born Again Believers, we must follow the footsteps of our LORD JESUS CHRIST. The reason they called them "CHRISTIANS" was because they behaved just like Jesus Christ Himself. *And the disciples were called Christians first in Antioch.* (Acts 11:26)

If you serve GOD, there must be PROOF in your life. *Then shall ye return, and discern between the righteous and the wicked, between him that serveth God and him that serveth him not.* (Malachi 3:18)

WHAT DOES IT MEAN TO BE IN CHRIST?

And he saith unto them, Follow me, and I will make you fishers of men.
Matthew 4:19

The word CHRIST means anointing. We cannot follow the anointed one and not become anointed also, by Him.

But the anointing which ye have received of Him abideth in you, and ye need not that any man teach you: but as the same anointing teacheth you of all things, and is truth, and is no lie, and even as it hath taught you, ye shall abide in Him.
1 John 2:27

To be IN CHRIST means to **behave** like Christ, to be **sharpened** by Christ. *Iron sharpeneth iron; so a man sharpeneth the countenance of his friend.* (Proverbs 27:17) The Bible recorded that when Saul came among the prophets, he prophesied. *And when they came thither to the hill, behold, a company of prophets met him; and the Spirit of God came upon him, and he prophesied among them.* (1 Samuel 10:10) In my opinion, as **believers** we must be in **command**. *I have been young, and now am old; yet have I not seen the righteous forsaken, nor his seed begging bread.* (Psalms 37:25) We must all carry the mentality of winners and not the mindset of beggars.

As a CHILD OF GOD, you should never be stranded nor SEEK the help of MAN, regardless of your prevailing situation. *Except the Lord build the house, they labour in vain that build it: except the Lord keep the city, the watchman waketh but in vain. It is vain for you to rise up early, to sit up late, to eat the bread of sorrows: for so he giveth his beloved sleep.* (Psalms 127:1-2)

To be IN CHRIST means to be genuinely planted in the house of God from the heart—and not by mouth confession only—i.e., "fake utterance" (false confession). This includes practicing **righteousness** as a lifestyle. Loving your neighbor as yourself. Doing what is **right** in the sight of GOD and in the sight of men. So many people in the faith have embarrassed themselves—ended up in jail for corruption, sexual scandal, embezzlement, alcohol and drug abuse, adultery, etc.

*Wherefore the Lord said, Forasmuch as
this people draw near me with their mouth,
and with their lips do honour me, but have removed
their heart far from me, and their fear toward me
is taught by the precept of men.*
Isaiah 29:13

Although so many good Christian's desire to walk in the reality of new birth, it will take the new anointing to operate and walk in the newness of life. There are strongholds designed to stop us. Among these strongholds are sinful habits, demonic agents policing and remote controlling our lives. The stronghold of sin, for example, has the power to **hinder** us as believers from experiencing the reality of new birth. Unless we deal with such habits, we will never experience the reality of new birth.

It will take a stronger power (JESUS CHRIST) to disarm the stronghold of demons and to disarm all evil forces keeping us from experiencing the reality of new birth.

*For that which I do I allow not: for what I would,
that do I not; but what I hate, that do I.*
Romans 7:15

*I returned, and saw under the sun, that the race
is not to the swift, nor the battle to the strong,
neither yet bread to the wise, nor yet riches
to men of understanding, nor yet favour to men
of skill; but time and chance happeneth to them all.*
Ecclesiastes 9:11

As **commanded**, it takes a **genuine prayer** and **fasting** to God for us to comprehend the hidden mysteries resisting us from doing the **right thing in life** (**practicing righteousness**).

Apostle Paul lamented:

*For the good that I would I do not:
but the evil which I would not, that I do.*
Romans 7:19

Have you really repented and given your heart not your lip to Jesus?

ARE YOU LIVING A RIGHTEOUS LIFESTYLE?

We ought to understand how these mysteries work. Unless we give up sin in our lives, God cannot use us. *If a man therefore purge himself from these, he shall be a vessel unto honour, sanctified, and meet for the master's use, and prepared unto every good work.* (2 Timothy 2:21) As long as we practice righteousness as a lifestyle, we are righteous before **Him**.

As simple as sin can be defined, when we repeat over and over the sin that easily besets us, we are actually swallowing our vomit. As far as I know, only dogs return to its own **vomit**. *But it is happened unto them according to the true proverb, The dog is turned to his own vomit again; and the sow that was washed to her wallowing in the mire.* (2 Peter 2:22) *As a dog returneth to his vomit, so a fool returneth to his folly.* (Proverbs 26:11)

The constant repetition of the sin that easily besets us, the sin we commit over and over is what we call **iniquity**. But GOD **promised** in Jeremiah 31:34, *"for I will forgive their iniquity, and I will remember their sin no more."*

Unless otherwise stated, until we resist the devil and submit ourselves-unto God, evil forces have the power to prevail over our lives. *Submit yourselves therefore to God. Resist the devil, and he will flee from you.* (James 4:7)

> *For God hath not given us the spirit of fear;*
> *but of power, and of love, and of a sound.*
> **2 Timothy 1:7**

The foundation to walk in the newness of life is a **sound mind**. But if the foundation be destroyed, what shall the righteous do? Jesus said in 2 Corinthians 3:11, *"For other foundation can no man lay than that is laid, which is Jesus Christ."*

What does this mean?

When we are not truly engrafted in CHRIST, we live under a faulty foundation. Unless we repent and renew our mind in Christ Jesus, evil forces have the power to prevail in our life. We will never experience the **baptism of fire and power**.

Unless we destroy our sinful lifestyle and accept the gift of **salvation**, we will never become outstanding in life. The word says in John 17:17—*sanctify them through thy truth: thy word is truth*. Our **heart** must be jealously guarded against all the wiles and schemes of the devil.

THE HOLY SPIRIT

Every Christian experience, conversion, baptism of fire or speaking in tongues is through the help of the Holy Spirit. We must respect and honor the **power & presence** of the Holy Spirit in our lives.

HOW TO ACTIVATE THE HOLY SPIRIT IN YOUR LIFE

1) First of all, we must believe that there IS a Holy Spirit.

2) Acknowledge the person of the Holy Spirt.

3) Believe in the ministration of the Holy Spirit.

4) Submit and obey the person of the Holy Spirit.

5) Welcome the sweet presence of the Holy Spirit.

We must appreciate the person of the **Holy Spirit** before we can ever begin **walking in the newness of life**.

Therefore if any man be in Christ,
he is a new creature: old things are passed away;
behold, all things are become new.
2 Corinthians 5:17

Regardless of my preaching and teaching, it is the Holy Spirit who will bring **conviction** and **judgement** to everyone. We must all learn to respect the help of the Holy Spirit in our lives.

Suffer not thy mouth to cause thy flesh to sin;
neither say thou before the angel, that it was
an error: wherefore should God be angry at thy voice,
and destroy the work of thine hands?
Ecclesiastes 5:6

DO NOT OFFEND THE HOLY SPIRIT WITH THE WORDS OF YOUR MOUTH

Beware of him, and obey his voice, provoke him not; for he will not pardon your transgressions: for my name is in him. But if thou shalt indeed obey his voice, and do all that I speak; then I will be an enemy unto thine enemies, and an adversary unto thine adversaries.
Exodus 23:21-22

No man can change what you believe or change your lifestyle but the Holy Spirit. The Holy Spirit, therefore, demands holiness, respect, quietness, meditation, rightesouness, faith, hope, trust and joy, etc.

> *Keep thy heart with all diligence;*
> *for out of it are the issues of life.*
> **Proverbs 4:23**

Every one of us engages our mind daily to work, to think, to mediate and to reflect. For example, every time we constantly think rich thoughts and put those thoughts into action, we become successful (RICH IN LIFE). It's the same when we engage our mind in poverty thoughts—we end up poor in life.

Unless we turn to the Almighty God and renew our mind, our life is heading to hell fire. Our thinking changes once we receive the word of GOD freely and willingly from the heart. *And be not conformed to this world: but be ye transformed by the renewing of your mind, that ye may prove what is that good, and acceptable, and perfect, will of God.* (Romans 12:2)

> *And even as they did not like to retain*
> *God in their knowledge, God gave them over to*
> *a reprobate mind, to do those things*
> *which are not convenient.*
> **Romans 1:28**

It is from the abundance of our heart that our

mouth speaks. The Bible says as a man thinketh, so is he. I used to know a very decent fellow who made up his mind to play ignorant of the consequences of breaking the laws of the United States. He ended up in jail because of the way he was thinking. *And be renewed in the spirit of your mind.* (Ephesians 4:23)

SOME STATES OF THE MIND AS ILLUSTRATED IN THE BIBLE

1) ***Evil Consience:*** This is a mindset that is constantly rejoicing over any evil work. Those who harbor this mindset take pleasure when evil is prevailing in the lives of men and women. The set of people with an evil conscience live with evil all their lives in their heart. All they can think and imagine in their life and in the lives of people around them is always of evil thoughts. In Hebrews 10:22 the Bible says, *"Let us draw near with a true heart in full assurance of faith, having our heart sprinkled from an evil conscience, and our bodies washed with pure water."*

2) ***Blind Mind:*** Those with a blind mindset cannot see any future for themselves and in the lives of others. This set of people do not believe in the validity of the power of the gospel. Satan has blinded their eyes lest they see any good in anything at all. This set of people constantly complain and murmur why things are not moving. These people are never grateful for what the Lord has done in their lives. They are greedy people

who constantly crave more and are never satisfied or happy with themselves and what they have accomplished in life. The Bible says in 2 Corinthians 4:4, *"In whom the God of this world hath blinded the minds of them which believe not, lest the light of the image of God, should shine unto them."*

3) **Dead Conscience:** Those with a dead conscience do not believe in the shedding blood of Jesus. This set of people visit the fetish priest and seek alternative solutions to their woes. For example, in 1 Samuel 28:7-8 King Saul deviated from God and pursued a familiar spirit and wizard as an alternative for the help of God Almighty, who made him a king and captain over his inheritance. *How much more shall the blood of Christ who through the eternal Spirit offered himself without spot to God, purge your conscience from dead works to serve the living God?* (Hebrew 9:14)

4) **Good Conscience:** Those who harbor good conscience are good people. They think and reflect well for themselves and for others. This set of people practice righteousness. They know God and follow the ways of God. These people want to serve God with their lives. They want to please God and to please their fellow men and brethren. *Holding faith and a good conscience; which some having put away concerning faith have made a shipwreck.* (1 Timothy1:18) *And Paul earnestly beholding the council, said Men and brethren, I have lived in all good conscience before God until this day.* (Acts 23:1) Apostle

Paul went further to explain in Acts 24:16, *"And herein do I exercise myself, to have always **a conscience void of offense towards God and towards men**."*

WHAT IS SIN?

One man said S.I.N means Satan Identification Number, but it is incomplete in my own interpretation. In my own definition, sin is disobeying God's words and commandments. Every time you operate outside of the commandment of God, you are committing sin. *He that committeth sin is of the devil; for the devil sinneth from the beginning. For this purpose the Son of God was manifested, that he might destroy the works of the devil.* (1 John 3:8)

Know ye not, that to whom ye yield yourselves servants to obey, his servants ye are to whom ye obey; whether of sin unto death, or of obedience unto righteousness.
Romans 6:16

The only alternative to destroy the stronghold of sin is RIGHTEOUSNESS. As simple as sin may appear, it has greater unseen **power** that enforces and rules anyone who submits to it. We must all deal with the sin that easily besets us in life

*Be not overcome of evil,
but overcome evil with good.*

Although we were born in sin, we should not allow sin to **dominate** our lives. David said in Psalms 51:3, *"For I acknowledge my transgressions and my sin is ever before me."* We must not take the purpose of the coming, life and death of Jesus in vain. Sin took over our lives from the days of Adam and Eve (SINNED). David attested in Psalms 51:5—*Behold I was shapen in iniquity; and in sin did my mother conceive me.*

WHO IS A SINNER?

There is a *stronger power* that pushes us all into a sinful lifestyle. Until such forces are crushed, it has the power to prevail over the life of the believer. In the subject of who is a sinner, there is no exemption—everyone is included. Is there any hidden sinful lifestyle you are dealing with? Confess it and crush it in the open with prayers.

Examine yourselves, whether ye be in the faith; prove your own selves. Know ye not your own selves, how that Jesus Christ is in you, except ye be reprobates?
2 Corinthians 13:5

Although most faith people live in denial about the work of the flesh, from my own scriptural understanding, everyone operating within the scope of Galatians 5:19-21 is classified as a sinner.

Now the works of the flesh are manifest, which are these; Adultery, fornication, uncleanness, lasciviousness, idolatry, witchcraft, hatred, variance, emulations, wrath, strife, seditions, heresies, envyings, murders, drunkenness, revellings, and such like: of the which I tell you before, as I have also told you in time past, that they which do such things shall not inherit the kingdom of God.
Galatians 5:19-21

Further supporting scripture…

But the fearful, and unbelieving, and the abominable, and murderers, and whoremongers, and sorcerers, and idolaters, and all liars, shall have their part in the lake which burneth with fire and brimstone: which is the second death.
Revelation 21:8

WHO, THEREFORE, IS A SINNER?

1) The Lazy Man: It is sinful for any able-bodied man or woman to fold their hands and make themselves beggars. The Bible says, *"the sluggard will not plow by reason of the cold; therefore shall he beg in harvest, and have nothing."* (Proverbs 20:4) In my own understanding, laziness is a sin. *For even when we were with you, this we commanded you, that if any would not work, neither should he eat.* (2 Thessalonians 3:10) Covenant mentality demands that we all understand that God has done His part over our lives. Jesus said I must work. It is dignified for every believer to earn money through the work of their hands—although most lazy people live in denial and tend to blame someone else. Nevertheless, Godliness demands that we take absolute responsibility for the outcome of our lives.

2) Unbelievers: In my own view, all that have not acknowledged Jesus Christ as Lord and savior are sinners. The Bible says God heareth not sinners. Without contradiction, all unbelievers live in a sinful lifestyle. Unless God has mercy, most unbelievers will not make eternity in heaven.

3) Lies: All lies are sinners before the Almighty God. Lying is a very serious sin, simply because it leads to poverty and shame. Lying decays great destiny and erodes potential future. Someone whom I know very well lies so much to themselves they became a beggar by paralyzing their future, frustrating the will of God over their life.

HOW DO I COME OUT OF SIN?

As a new convert (BELIEVERS), the compelling urge to sin will not casually go away. We must consciously engage in warfare and break the stronghold of sin (the old man of sin). For anyone to come out of **sin**, first there must be a **willing heart**. For anyone to come out of sin, it must be our own personal **choice**—

not someone else persuading us to come out of sin..

You must **REPENT**—then **CONFESS & PROCLAIM** the LORD JESUS CHRIST.

The word says, *"as many as received him, to them gave he power to become the sons of God, even to them that believe on his name."* (John 1:12)

To qualify for divine visitation, do the following sincerely:

1) Acknowledge that you are a sinner and that He died for you. (Romans 3:23)

2) Repent of your sins. (Acts 3:19, Luke 13:5, 2 Peter 3:9)

3) Believe in your heart that Jesus died for your sin. (Romans 10:10)

4) Confess Jesus as the Lord over your life. (Romans 10:10, Acts 2:21)

NOW REPEAT THIS PRAYER AFTER ME:

"Lord Jesus, I accept you today as my Lord and my savior. Forgive me of my sins, wash me with your blood. Right now, I believe I am sanctified, I am saved, I am free. I am free from the power of sin to serve the Lord Jesus. Thank you, Lord, for saving me. Amen."

Congratulations.

YOU ARE NOW A BORN AGAIN CHRISTIAN!

STEPS TO OVERCOME THE LIFESTYLE OF SIN

1) REPENT: Unless otherwise stated, until we repent, confess and believe the LORD JESUS CHRIST, sin will easily beset our lives.

2) FAITH: It is our faith in GOD that will grant us the willpower to overcome a sinful lifestyle.

3) DECISIONS: Everybody knows that when we make up our mind concerning certain things in our lives, good things happen. So make up your mind to stop the sin that easily besets you. Take a decision today and evict the old man of sin. (See Romans 6:1-14).

4) PRAYER: Without prayer we will still be confused about our roots in Jesus Christ. As long as you develop a prayer lifestyle, you will not easily fall victim to the sin that easily besets you.

SUMMARY OF CHAPTER ONE

We must appreciate the person of the Holy Spirit before we can begin **walking in the newness of life**.

Therefore if any man be in Christ,
he is a new creature: old things are passed away;
behold, all things are become new.
2 Corinthians 5:17

Regardless of my preaching and teaching, it is the Holy Spirit who will bring **conviction** and **judgement** to everyone. We must all learn to respect the help of the Holy Spirit in our lives.

Suffer not thy mouth to cause thy flesh to sin;
neither say thou before the angel,
that it was an error: wherefore should God
be angry at thy voice, and destroy
the work of thine hands?
Ecclesiastes 5:6

DO NOT OFFEND THE HOLY SPIRIT WITH THE WORDS OF YOUR MOUTH

Beware of him, and obey his voice, provoke him not; for he will not pardon your transgressions: for my name is in him. But if thou shalt indeed obey his voice, and do all that I speak; then I will be an enemy unto thine enemies, and an adversary unto thine adversaries.
Exodus 23:21-22

No man can change what you believe or change your lifestyle but the Holy Spirit. The Holy Spirit, therefore, demands holiness, respect, quietness, meditation, rightesouness, faith, hope, trust and joy, etc.

CHAPTER 2
UNDERSTANDING THE NEW ANOINTING

*But my horn shalt thou exalt like the horn of an unicorn:
I shall be anointed with fresh oil.*
Psalms 92:10

Everyone has the opportunity to experience the new anointing, especially at new birth. Perhaps you have never experienced the anointing of God at NEW BIRTH—when you became a Born Again Christian—or at any stage of your **spiritual walk** with Jesus. The truth is, new birth is a newfound life. At new birth, we experience the Holy Ghost and Jesus Christ Himself.

*Jesus answered and said unto him, Verily, verily,
I say unto thee, Except a man be born again,
he cannot see the kingdom of God.*
John 3:3

The anointing we experience at new birth, (BORN AGAIN EXPERIENCE) is the new anointing that turns our lives around. It converts our person into another man (SPIRIT BORN). *That which is born of the flesh is flesh; and that which is born of the Spirit is spirit.* (John 3:6)

We will never become a genuine new creature

unless there is a transformation in our spiritual system. *And be not conformed to this world: but be ye transformed by the renewing of your mind, that ye may prove what is that good, and acceptable, and perfect, will of God.* (Romans 12:2)

No genuine conversion will take place without a genuine encounter and experience. Until there is a real transformation and a genuine conversion we will never become a new creature. There are many people in the church but they are not in Christ.

Therefore if any man be in Christ,
he is a new creature: old things are passed away;
behold, all things are become new.
2 Corinthians 5:17

WHAT DOES IT MEAN TO BE IN CHRIST?

Jesus answered, Verily, verily, I say unto thee,
Except a man be born of water and of the Spirit,
he cannot enter into the kingdom of God.
That which is born of the flesh is flesh;
and that which is born of the Spirit is spirit.
John 3:5-6

Consider the above scripture. Too many believers have questioned the reality of new birth. At new birth there must be a conversion, a real experience and a transformation with the help of the **Holy Spirit**. Oftentimes some believers respond to altar calls because of the financial and material challenges facing them. Some other believers respond to altar calls because the pastor asked them to come forward or a family member persuaded them to do it. The Bible says in Isaiah 29:13—*Wherefore the Lord said, Forasmuch as this people draw near me with their mouth, and with their lips do honour me, but have removed their heart far from me, and their fear toward me is taught by the precept of men.* I admonish you to desire a real encounter with Jesus.

Understand that it is the will of God to genuinely grant you a real **encounter & experience** at new birth with the **help of the Holy Spirit**. Therefore do not fake your conversion experience and the annointing of God. No genuine transformation will take place without a supernatural encounter by the Holy Ghost.

Below is Saul's transformation encounter with Jesus *before he became Paul*.

And as he journeyed, he came near Damascus:
and suddenly there shined round about him
a light from heaven: And he fell to the earth,
and heard a voice saying unto him,
Saul, Saul, why persecutest thou me?
Acts 9:3-4

The dynamics and mystery of the new anointing is revealed only by the **Holy Spirit**. So many people do not understand what it means when we talk about

being born of the Spirit of God. The reality of new birth means that we have experienced Jesus Christ in a new dimension. Like the above scripture, Paul experienced the Lord Jesus by this great encounter on his way to Damascus.

Let me say it bold here—there is nothing that refreshes like the new anointing that is new birth. The Bible says in Romans 10:1, *"For with the heart man believeth unto righteousness; and with the mouth confession is made unto salvation."*

I admonish you to **repent** of your **sins** and **evil ways**. The Bible teaches that only dogs return to their vomit. *As a dog returneth to his vomit, so a man returneth to his folly.* (Proverbs 26:11)

Every time we "**repent**, GOD is bound to **restore** our lives." No man will be able to operate in the realm of the new anointing without the help of the Holy Spirit.

CHAPTER 3
THE BENEFIT OF THE NEW ANOINTING

Then Samuel took a vial of oil, and poured it upon his head, and kissed him, and said, Is it not because the LORD hath anointed thee to be captain over his inheritance.
1 Samuel 10:1

It is proven that Christian leaders are the best leaders in world history. All Christian leaders are anointing to do righteously and to execute the power and the law committed into their hands. Most Christian leaders are guided by the fear of God.

The new anointing guarantees and provides divine direction from the Almighty God of Jacob. The Bible says in Proverbs 16:12 that *"it is abomination for kings to do wickedness: for the throne is established by righteousness.* In Proverbs 25:5, the Bible says, *"Take away the wicked from before the king, and his throne shall be established in righteousness."*

BENEFITS OF NEW BIRTH-NEW ANOINTING:

1) **Possession** of the Spirit of the Lord. *And the Spirit of the LORD will come upon thee*. (1 Samuel 10:6)

2) **Empowerment** into the supernatural realm. *And thou shalt prophesy with them, and shalt be turned into another man.* (1 Samuel 10:6)

3) **Unlimited access** into higher spiritual things. *And that which is born of the Spirit is spirit.* (John 3:6)

4) Accurate **discernment** into spiritual things. *But the natural man receiveth not the things of the Spirit of God: for they are foolishness unto him: neither can he know them, because they are spiritually discerned.* (1 Corinthians 2:14)

5) It is the **beginning steps** that will lead you into eternity. *Jesus answered and said unto him, Verily, verily, I say unto thee, Except a man be born again, he cannot see the kingdom of God.* (John 3:3)

6) It **provokes signs** and **protection** from the Almighty God. *And let it be, when these signs are come unto thee, that thou do as occasion serve thee; for God is with thee.* (1 Samuel 10:7)

7) **Protection**. Everyone with the new anointing enjoys the great backing of the great and mighty God of Jacob. The Bible says, *"touch not mine anointed and do my prophets no harm."* (1 Chronicles 16:22)

ACCESS TO RECIEVE THE PERSON OF THE HOLY SPIRIT

1) BE BORN AGAIN: In these evil days full of terror, it is easy to tell when the un-believer is going through trials and tribulations. As long as you are not a born again Christian all you will get is "sorriooo" and a mere word of comfort—"It is well with you." Of course you know it shall not be well with you. We established earlier that the Holy Spirit does not lead sinners. The Spirit of the Lord comes afresh and becomes a reality once you confess Jesus Christ as your Lord and savior. *Jesus answered and said unto him, Verily, verily, I say unto thee, Except a man be born again, he cannot see the kingdom of God. Nicodemus saith unto him, How can a man be born when he is old? can he enter the second time into his mother's womb, and be born? Jesus answered, Verily, verily, I say unto thee, Except a man be born of water and of the Spirit, he cannot enter into the kingdom of God. That which is born of the flesh is flesh; and that which is born of the Spirit is spirit. Marvel not that I said unto thee, Ye must be born again. The wind bloweth where it listeth, and thou hearest the sound thereof, but canst not tell whence it cometh, and whither it goeth: so is every one that is born of the Spirit.* (John 3:3-8) Until you confess and acknowledge the Lord Jesus as your savior, you will forever be subdued with trials and tribulations. Eternity is real, therefore if you are not a born again Christian, do so quickly before concluding this Holy Spirit revealed manual.

2) THE FEAR OF GOD: You must develop the consciousness of the fear of God in your heart if you desire to overcome trials and tribulations. As long as you fear God, the help of the Holy Spirit is on the way. The Lord made it clear it shall be well with the righteous, but it shall not be well with the wicked. *Though a sinner do evil an hundred times, and his days be prolonged, yet surely I know that it shall be well with them that fear God, which fear before him: But it shall not be well with the wicked, neither shall he prolong his days, which are as a shadow; because he feareth not before God.* (Ecclesiastes 8:12-13) The Holy Spirit will choose you, to teach you all things once you embrace the fear of God in your life. *What man is he that feareth the Lord? him shall he teach in the way that he shall choose.* (Psalm 25:12)

3) RIGHTEOUS LIFESTYLE: As long as you practice a righteous lifestyle, you will forever enjoy the presence of the Holy Spirit. *Little children, let no man deceive you: he that doeth righteousness is righteous, even as he is righteous.* (1 John 3:7) *And the work of righteousness shall be peace; and the effect of righteousness quietness and assurance forever.* (Isaiah 32:17) Righteousness is the access key to provoke the presence of the Holy Spirit.

4) INTEGRITY: In my own simplified words, the spirit of integrity is the truth. The Holy Spirit is the spirit of truth, therefore the Holy Spirit enjoys everyone who speaks and carries the mantle of the truth in their life. In this race of life, integrity is the access key to provoke the person of the Holy Spirit. *The integrity of the upright shall guide them.* (Proverbs 11:3)

5) AGREEMENT: The Bible asks, *"Can two walk to-*

gether unless they be agreed?" (Amos 3:3) Can two walk together, except they be agreed? Agreement is the access gateway for the person of the Holy Spirit. vs19-20 *But if he will not hear thee, then take with thee one or two more, that in the mouth of two or three witnesses every word may be established.* (Matthew 18:16) *Verily I say unto you, Whatsoever ye shall bind on earth shall be bound in heaven: and whatsoever ye shall loose on earth shall be loosed in heaven. Again I say unto you, That if two of you shall agree on earth as touching any thing that they shall ask, it shall be done for them of my Father which is in heaven. For where two or three are gathered together in my name, there am I in the midst of them.* (Matthew 18:18-20)

6) THE RIGHT WORDS: Every time you speak the right word, the Holy Spirit comes into your life. Job 6:25 declares, *"How forcible are right words!"* Jesus said there is no idle word in the kingdom. Every time you speak, your words are judged by the angels of the living God. *Suffer not thy mouth to cause thy flesh to sin; neither say thou before the angel, that it was an error: wherefore should God be angry at thy voice, and destroy the work of thine hands?* (Ecclesiastes 5:6) The right words will bring you out of captivity, the right word will provoke the Holy Spirit to come to your rescue.

7) SOUL WINNING: Until you join forces with Jesus to enforce the great commission to win souls for His kingdom, the Holy Spirit will forever be far from you. *And Jesus came and spake unto them, saying, All power is* *given unto me in heaven and in earth. Go ye therefore, and teach all nations, baptizing them in the name of the Father, and of the Son, and of the Holy Ghost: Teaching them to observe all things whatsoever I have commanded you: and, lo, I am with you always, even unto the end of the world. Amen.* (Matthew 28:18-20)

8) OBEDIENCE: As long as you are walking in disobedience, you will never experience the manifestation of the Holy Spirit. Remember he is the seal of redemption. *In whom ye also trusted, after that ye heard the word of truth, the gospel of your salvation: in whom also after that ye believed, ye were sealed with that holy Spirit of promise.* (Ephesians 1:13) *Obey them that have the rule over you, and submit yourselves: for they watch for your souls, as they that must give account, that they may do it with joy, and not with grief: for that is unprofitable for you. (*Hebrews 13:17)

9) PRAY IN THE SPIRIT: When you pray in the SPIRIT you are not speaking to men but unto GOD. *For he that speaketh in an unknown tongue speaketh not unto men, but unto God: for no man understandeth him; howbeit in the spirit he speaketh mysteriest.* (1 Corinthians 14:2)

WAYS IN WHICH THE HOLY SPIRIT LEADS & DIRECTS US

AUDIBLE VOICE: The Holy Spirit speaks to us. The Bible says in Acts 10:19, *"while Peter thought on the vision the Holy Spirit said unto him, Behold three men seek thee.*

And then there was this—*As they ministered to the Lord, and fasted, the Holy Ghost said, Separate me Barnabas and Saul for the work whereunto I have called them. If you are not in the Spirit you can get into the spirit by singing a heavenly song unto the Holy Spirit.* (Acts 13:2) This I called melody.

MELODY: Every time you sing unto the Lord, you are bound to hear His voice in a song or melody—through singing sweet songs late at night or early in the morning. *And the Lord shall cause his glorious voice to be heard, and shall shew the lighting down of his arm, with the indignation of his anger, and with the flame of a devouring fire, with scattering, and tempest, and hailstones. For through the voice of the Lord shall the Assyrian be beaten down, which smote with a rod.* (Isaiah 30:29) *For the Lord shall comfort Zion: he will comfort all her waste places; and he will make her wilderness like Eden, and her desert like the garden of the Lord; joy and gladness shall be found therein, thanksgiving, and the voice of melody.* (Isaiah 51:3) You provoke the Holy Spirit into action once you lift up spiritual songs to minister to the Spirit. *While Peter yet spake these words, the Holy Ghost fell on all them which heard the word.* (Acts 10:44)

CHAPTER 4
WALKING IN THE REALITY OF NEW BIRTH

*He that walketh with wise men shall be wise:
but a companion of fools shall be destroyed.*
Proverbs 13:20

According to 1 Timothy 1:17, as long as you walk with the only wise God, you are insured to walk in wisdom—as long as you have truly repented and given your life to Jesus Christ. It is established that Jesus did great and mighty things in his days. Abram was strong and became great because he, Abraham, walked with God. *And when Abram was ninety years old and nine, the Lord appeared to Abram, and said unto him, I am the Almighty God walk before me and be thou perfect.* (Genesis 17:1-2) Until you can accept the works of God and the blood of Jesus that was shed on the cross, you will never become a candidate for the reality of new birth.

WHAT DOES IT MEAN TO WALK IN THE REALITY OF NEW BIRTH?

*He that honor me, I will honor
and he that despised me I will lightly esteem.*
1 Samuel 2:30

God has given us the power of choice to worship Him and to choose whom we should serve. Oftentimes most church people forget the Lord and live their lives carelessly as they please. The reality of new birth is that it shapes our lives to please the Lord. So many people want to please the Lord and walk in righteousness the remaining days of their lives—but don't know how. Most believers forget that God is Spirit and often they only remember God only on Sundays or during midweek service.

The reality of new birth establishes that you must be conscious of the will and ways of God. You must develop fellowship with the assembly of believers. You must love your neighbor as yourself. It is an abomination in this end time when people who claim to know God commit so many atrocities that even the elected are misled by their gainsaying and doctrines.

THE DEMANDS FOR WALKING IN THE REALITY OF NEW BIRTH

1) FAITH: The Bible teaches that without faith, you and I cannot please the Lord. Do you have faith today—at least like a mustard seed? I encourage you to develop faith in God and in all you do in life. The Bible says whatever that is not done in faith is sin. Faith in God will allow you to see visions and revelations of the deep things of God. Faith in God guarantees you the sovereign power and authority of the Most High God.

2) GOOD CONSCIENCE: It takes a good conscience to walk in the reality of new birth. A true repented soul seeks and desires to please God and their fellow men. *Holding faith and a good conscience.* (1 Timothy 1:18) *And Paul earnestly beholding the council, said Men and brethren, I have lived in all good conscience before God until this day.* (Acts 23:1) Apostle Paul went further to explain in Acts 24:16, *"And herein do I exercise myself, to have always a conscience void of offense towards God and towards men."*

3) RIGHTEOUSNESS: It will take a righteous lifestyle to make heaven. Most people do not remember eternity. No one can make heaven with a wicked mindset. Until you change the way you think and behave, God will not have mercy nor guarantee you a place in eternity. Therefore, if you have not accepted the Lord, if you have not given your life to Jesus Christ, I will admonish you as you finish reading this book.

The following steps will help you become a Born Again Christian. To qualify for divine **salvation**, do the following sincerely:

1) Acknowledge that you are a sinner and that He died for you. (Romans 3:23)

2) Repent of your sins. (Acts 3:19, Luke 13:5, 2 Peter 3:9)

3) Believe in your heart that Jesus died for your sin.

(Romans 10:10)

4) Confess Jesus as the Lord over your life. (Romans 10:10, Acts2:21)

NOW REPEAT THIS PRAYER AFTER ME:

Say Lord Jesus, I accept you today, as my Lord and my savior, forgive me of my sins wash me with your blood. Right now, I believe, I am sanctified, I am saved, I am free, I am free from the power of sin to serve the Lord Jesus. Thank you Lord for saving me. Amen.

Congratulations.

YOU ARE NOW A BORN AGAIN CHRISTAIN!

Again, I say to you—congratulations! I adjure you to watch the Spirit of God bear witness with your Spirit confirming His word with signs following. The word says the Spirit itself beareth witness with our spirit, that we are the children of God.

DECISION KEYS

1) Nothing changes until you make up your mind.

2) Decision is the gateway to deliverance.

3) Until you decide, no one will decide for you.

4) Your prosperity is proportional to your decisions.

5) The decision you make will determine the future you will create

6) Decision creates future and fulfills destinies.

7) Decision beautifies our future.

8) Decision keeps you out of trouble.

9) Decision exempts you from evil.

10) Decision gurantees eternity.

11) You can only go far in life by your faith decisions.

12) You are poor because you made such decisions

13) Make a decision and change your life.

14) Life changing decisions are a function of quality

information.

15) Success in life is a function of decision.

16) Life experiences are full of decisions.

17) Decisions change destinies.

18) Never settle for information—always look for revelation.

19) You are where you are today based on your last decision.

20) Information is crucial in decision making.

21) Decision makers rule the world.

22) You can rule your world with quality decisions.

23) As long as you decide rightly, Satan cannot harrass you.

PRAYER POINTS OVERCOME TRIALS BY THE HELP OF THE HOLY SPIRIT

1) Father Lord, deliver me from this present trial, in the Name of Jesus.

2) Almighty Father, break me out of this present obscurity, in the Name of Jesus.

3) Holy Spirit, help me to overcome this trial, in Jesus Name.

4) Holy Spirit, speak to me, in the Name of Jesus.

5) Holy Spirit, minister to my subconscious spirit, in the Name of Jesus.

6) Fire of God, burn down every mountain of difficulty, in the Name of Jesus.

7) Holy Ghost, baptize me with your fire, in the Name of Jesus.

8) Holy Spirit, go before me and favor me in this present challenge, in the Name of Jesus.

9) Spirit of God, grant me liberty and freedom by the fire of the Holy Spirit, in the Name of Jesus.

10) Father Lord, intervene on my behalf, in the Name

of Jesus.

11) Ancient of day, liberate me this season, in the Name of Jesus.

12) Immortal redeemer, bring me higher above these prevailing changes.

13) Lord God, turn this present obstacale into my miracle, in the Name of Jesus.

14) Fire of God, break down these obstacles for me, in the Name of Jesus.

15) Holy Spirit, favor me in, Jesus Name.

16) Holy Spirit. release me from this challenge, in the Name of Jesus.

17) Holy Spirit, become my compionion, in Jesus Name.

18) Holy Spirit, represent me in this matter.

19) Holy Spirit, elevant me beyond my own immagination, in the Name of Jesus.

20) Holy Spirit, do not allow my enemies to truimph over my life, in the Name of Jesus.

21) Fire of God, protect me, in the Name of Jesus.

22) Fire of God, destroy my enemies, in the Name of Jesus.

23) Fire of God, build a wall around me, in the Name of Jesus.

24) Fire of God, expose my enemies, in the Name of Jesus.

25) Fire of God, prove yourself, in the Name of Jesus.

26) Holy Spirit, represent me in jesus name.

27) Holy Spirit, release your boldnes into my life.

28) Holy Spirit, grant me signs and wonders.

29) Holy Spirit, make me a living wonder in my lifetime.

30) Holy Spirit, turn my life around, in the Name of Jesus.

31) Holy Spirit, I will not remain at this level, in the Name of Jesus.

32) Spirit of God, lift me higher, in the mighty Name of Jesus.

33) Angels of God, minister unto me, in the Name of Jesus.

34) Hand of God, separate me this season, in the Name of Jesus.

CONCLUSION

Jesus answered and said unto him, Verily, verily, I say unto thee, Except a man be born again, he cannot see the kingdom of God. Nicodemus saith unto him, How can a man be born when he is old? can he enter the second time into his mother's womb, and be born? Jesus answered, Verily, verily, I say unto thee, Except a man be born of water and of the Spirit, he cannot enter into the kingdom of God.
John 3:5

Oftentimes, we lie to ourselves. Tell yourself the truth and walk in the reality of the revealed truth.

But seek ye first the kingdom of God, and his righteousness; and all these things shall be added unto you.
Matthew 6:33

As you conclude this book, I admonish you to seek first the kingdom of God, and all other things will be added into your life.

Let us hear the conclusion of the whole matter:
Fear God, and keep his commandments:
for this is the whole duty of man.
For God shall bring every work into judgment,
with every secret thing, whether it be good,
or whether it be evil
Ecclesiastes 12:13-14

All you have read remains a story until there is a quickening transformation inside of your heart. The mysteries of God are provoked only when you FEAR GOD and keep His commandments. The Bible says in Ecclesiastes 12:14—*For God shall bring every work into judgment, with every secret thing, whether it be good, or whether it be evil*. If you are a Born Again Christian, we'd like to encourage you in your Christian life. If you are not a Born Again Christian, we can help you here receive genuine salvation.

Therefore if any man be in Christ, he is a new creature:
old things are passed away; behold, all things
are become new.
2 Corinthians 5:17

WHAT MUST I DO TO DETERMINE MY DIVINE VISITATION?

To determine divine visitation you must be born again! The word says as many as received Him, to them gave He power to become the sons of God.

Even to them that believe on His name.

To qualify for divine visitation, do the following sincerely:

1) Acknowledge that you are a sinner and that He died for you. (Romans 3:23)

2) Repent of your sins. (Acts 3:19, Luke 13:5, 2 Peter 3:9)

3) Believe in your heart that Jesus died for your sin. (Romans 10:10)

4) Confess Jesus as the Lord over your life. (Romans 10:10, Acts 2:21)

NOW REPEAT THIS PRAYER AFTER ME:

"Lord Jesus, I accept you today as my Lord and my savior. Forgive me of my sins, wash me with your blood. Right now, I believe I am sanctified, I am saved, I am free. I am free from the power of sin to serve the Lord Jesus. Thank you, Lord, for saving me. Amen."

Congratulations.

YOU ARE NOW A BORN AGAIN CHRISTIAN!

Again, I say to you—congratulations!

I adjure you to watch the Spirit of God bear witness with your spirit confirming His word with signs following. The word says The Spirit itself beareth witness with our spirit, that we are the children of God. Join a Bible-believing church or join us on our weekly and Sunday worship services at 343 Sanford Ave., Newark, New Jersey 07106.

WISDOM KEYS

— Every productive society is a society heading to the top.

—Millions of Nigerians run away from Nigeria. Very few Nigerians stay in Nigeria.

—My decision to return Nigeria is the will of God for my life.

—My shortcoming in America after 18 years is the fact that I've trained me to be wise, to think, reflect and reason appropriately.

—If you train your mind to reason, it will train your hands to earn money.

—It is absurd to use the money of the heathen to build the kingdom of the living God.

—Every ministry reveals its agenda and VISION either at the beginning or at the end.

—Be careful of your life. It is your first ministry.

—The average American mind is conditioned for a continual quest to get new things and discard the old.

—When I considered well, my BMW jeep became my initial deposit for the work of the ministry in Nigeria.

—Money will never fall from any tree or person. Make up your mind to be independent today.

—Everyone is waiting for you to change your mind. Until you change your thinking, nothing changes around you.

—Multiple academic degrees in other disciplines gave me the chance to think and reason.

—Whatever anyone is thinking at any time reveals what is inside of their heart.

—All planned events are the product of meditation.

—Every event is designed for a designated timeline.

—Wisdom is your ability to think, to create and invent.

— If you can think wisely enough, you will come out of debt.

—The distance between you and your success is your innovative and creative ability to think well.

—Success is the result of hard work, commitment, resolve and determined learning from past mistakes and failings.

—If you organize your mind, you have organized your life and destiny.

—There is a thin line between success and failure.

—Wealth is your ability to think, power is your ability to reason and success is your ability to be informed.

—If you can make use of your mind by thinking and reasoning, God will make use of your life and destiny.

—Reflect, reason, think and be Great.

—Famous people are born of woman.

—That you will make it is your intention, that you will survive is your resolve, that you will succeed with changes is your determination, personal efforts and hard work.

—No man was born a failure.

—Lack of vision is the result of failure.

—Working with mental patients encourages and aspire me to be a productive observant and dedicated to my assignment.

—Successful people are not magicians. It is the will-power, combined with hard work and determination and a resolve to succeed, that make them succeed.

—In the unequivocal state of the mind, intention is not a location or a position. It is the state of the mind.

—So many people think that they think.

—The mind is used to think, to reflect and to reason.

—You will remain blind with your eyes open until you can see with your mind by thinking.

—There is no favoritism in accurate and precise calculation.

—Although knowledge is power, information is the key and gateway to a great future.

—It will take the hand of God to move the hand of man.

—With the backing of the great wise God, nothing will disconnect you from your inheritance.

—As long as you have wisdom and understanding of God, Satan and evil cannot manipulate your life and destiny.

—You have come this far in life by your own judgment and the decisions you made in the past. Now lean in and listen to God for another dimension of greatness.

—Great people are ordinary people. It is extra ordinary efforts and the price of sacrifice that produces greatness in them.

—As a mental direct care worker, I saw a great pastor and a motivational speaker within myself.

—A menial job does not reduce your self-worth. Until you resolve to achieve greatness and see greatness in all you do, you will never count in your community.

—The principle of Jesus will solve your gambling and addiction problems.

—The man of Jesus will lead you into heaven.

—Everyone has their self-appraisal and what they think about you. Until you discover yourself, other opinions about you will alter the real you.

—Supervisors and directors are just a position in the chain of command in a workplace. Never allow your supervisor hierarchy to alter your opinion of yourself.

—Everyone can come out of debt if they make up their mind.

—The fact that I am not a decision-maker at work does not diminish my contribution to my world.

—Although it appears like it was a poor decision to accept a direct care employment at a psychiatric hospital, as I reflect on my nine years of that experience, it became apparent that I have learned and experienced enough for my next assignment.

—Self-encouragement and determination is a resolve of the heart.

—If you are determined to make a difference and do the things that make a difference, you will eventually make a difference.

—Good things do not come easy.

—Short cuts will cut your life short.

—Those who look ahead move ahead.

—Life is all about making an impact. In your lifetime strive to make an impact in your community.

—Make friends and connect with people who are moving ahead of you in life.

—If you can look around well, you have come a long way in your life, made a lot of difference and realized a lot of success in life.

—If you are my old friend, hurry up to reach out to me before I become a stranger to you.

—I am blessed with inspirations from God that changed my interpretation of the world around me.

—I thought I was stagnant and lonely until I looked around and noticed my children running around and my wife cooking.

— At 40, I resigned my job to seek the Lord forever.

—My ministry took a drastic rise to the top when the wisdom of God visited me with knowledge and understanding.

—You will be a better person if you understand the characteristics of your personality like your mood swings, attitudes and habits.

—It is the seed of love you sow into the heart of a child and a woman that you reap in due time.

—Love is not selfish. Love shares everything, including the concealed secrets of the mind.

—As long as you have a prayer life and a Bible, you will never feel lonely in the race of life.

—When good friends disconnect from you, let them go. They might have seen something new in a different direction.

—Confidence in yourself and in God is the only way to bring you out of captivity

—Never train a child to waste his or her time.

—The mind is the greatest asset of a great future.

—You walk by common sense, run by principles and fly by instruction.

—Those who become successful in life did it by self-determination, hard work and learning from past failures.

—Most successful people are lonely people. No one renders help to them, believing they are already successful. Except when they seek for more knowledge and information, they are all alone.

— I have seen a towing truck vehicle. I have also seen a towing ship in the water. But I have never seen a towing airplane in the air.

—I exercise my judgment and make a decision every minute of the day. Decisions are crucial, critical and vital with reference to your future.

—So many people wish for a great future. You can only work towards a great future.

—Your celebrity status began when you discovered your talent. What are you good at? Work at it with all your commitment.

—Prayers will sustain you, but the wisdom of God will prosper you.

—When I met Oyedepo, his teachings changed my perspective. But when I met Ibiyeomie, his teachings changed my perception.

— I will be successful in ministry if only I concentrate and focus my energy in the work of the ministry.

— It took the late Dr. Norman Vincent Peale's book to open my mind towards the kingdom of success. *59) Enforcing Your Kingdom Rights*
60) Escaping the Traps of Immoralities
61) Escaping the Trap of Poverty
62) Accessing Biblical Prosperity
63) Accessing True Riches in Christ
64) Silencing the Voice of the Accuser
65) Overcoming the Forces of Oppositions
66) Quenching the Voice of the Avenger
67) Silencing Demonic Prediction & Projection
68) Silencing Your Mocker
69) Understanding the Power of the Holy Ghost

CHAPTER 5
PRAYER OF SALVATION

I am glad you have read this book all the way from the beginning to this point. All I have said from the beginning will remain a mystery until you commit it into practice.

And before you do so, I want you, if you have not given your life to Jesus yet, to do so now. Give your life to Christ. I want you to know the truth! The truth is that Jesus died for your sins. And because He died, you must be alive and prosperous.

WHAT MUST I DO TO DETERMINE GENUINE SALVATION?

To determine **genuine salvation**, we must be born again! The word says as many as received Him, to them gave He power to become the sons of God. Even to them that believe on His name.

Follow the proceeding steps:

1) Acknowledge that you are a sinner and that He died for you. (Romans 3:23)

2) Repent of your sins. (Acts 3:19, Luke 13:5, 2 Peter 3:9)

3) Believe in your heart that Jesus died for your sin. (Romans 10:10)

4) Confess Jesus as the Lord over your life. (Romans 10:10, Acts 2:21)

NOW REPEAT THIS PRAYER AFTER ME:

*Say Lord Jesus, I accept you today,
as my Lord and my savior, forgive me of my sins
wash me with your blood. Right now, I believe,
I am sanctified, I am save, I am free, I am free
from the power of sin to serve the Lord Jesus.
Thank you Lord for saving me. Amen.*

Congratulations.

YOU ARE NOW A BORN AGAIN CHRISTAIN!

Again, I say to you—congratulations!

I adjure you to watch the Spirit of God bear witness with your Spirit confirming His word with signs following. The word says the Spirit itself beareth witness with our spirit, that we are the children of God.

MIRACLE CARE OUTREACH

*"...But that the members should have
the same care one for another"*
1 Corinthians 12:25

We are all members of the body of Christ. Jesus commanded us to love our neighbor as ourselves. This includes caring for one another as a member of one body. True love is expressed in caring and giving. The word says, for God so Love He gave....

Reach out to someone in need of Jesus. Help someone in crisis find Christ. Look out and prove your love to Jesus by caring and inviting your friends and associates to find Jesus the Healer.

Invite your friends to our Home Care Cell Fellowship (Miracle Chapel Intl. Satellite Fellowship). We're in the U.S. at 33 Schley Street, Newark, New Jersey 07112. Home Care Cell Fellowship Group meets every Tuesday at 6:00pm-7:00pm.

If you are in Nigeria—MIRACLE OF GOD MINISTRIES, aka "MIRACLE CHAPEL INTL." Mpama–Egbu-Owerri Imo state Nigeria.

LIFE IS NOT ALL ABOUT DURATION, BUT IT'S ALL ABOUT DONATION

What does this statement mean?

| Chapter 5 | Prayer of Salvation |

Life consists not in accumulation of material wealth. (Luke 12:15) But it's all about liberality...i.e., what you can give and share with others. (Proverbs 11:25) When you live for others, you live forever—because you outlive your generation by the legacy you leave behind after you depart into glory to be with the Lord. But when you live for yourself, when you are reduced to SELF—you are easily forgotten when you die and depart in glory.

Permit me to admonish you today to live your life to be a blessing to a soul connected to you today. I want you to know that so many souls are connected and looking up to you, and through you so many souls will be saved and rescued from destruction. Will you disciple someone today to find Jesus Christ?

As a genuine Christian, it is your duty to evangelize Jesus Christ to all you meet on your way. Jesus is still in the healing business—Jesus is still doing miracles, from time of old to now. Therefore, tell someone about Jesus Christ today, disciple and bring them to Church. *Philip findeth Nathanael...* (John 1:45)

Please prove the sincerity of your love for God today, please become a soul winner. The dignity of your Christianity is hidden in your boldness to proclaim and evangelize Jesus Christ to all you meet on your way. There is a question mark on the integrity of your Christianity until you become a life soul winner. Invite someone to join us worship the Lord Jesus this coming Sunday. Amen.

MIRACLE OF GOD MINISTRIES
PILLARS OF THE COMMISSION

We Believe, Preach and Practice the following:

1) We believe and preach Salvation to every living human being.

2) We believe and preach Repentance and Forgiveness of sins.

3) We believe and preach the baptism of the Holy Spirit and Spiritual gifts.

4) We believe and teach Prosperity.

5) We believe and preach Divine Healing and Miracles—Signs and Wonder.

6) We believe and preach Faith.

7) We believe and proclaim the Power of God (Supernatural).

8) We believe and proclaim Praise and Worship to God.

9) We believe and preach Wisdom.

10) We believe and preach Holiness (Consecration).

11) We believe and preach Vision.

12) We believe and teach the Word of God.

13) We believe and teach Success.

14) We believe and practice Prayer.

15) We believe and teach Deliverance.

These 15 stones form the Pillars of Our Commission

MY HEARTFELT PRAYER FOR YOU

It is my burning desire for God to touch you through one of our teaching books or CDs. It also my personal desire for you encounter God for yourself.

Now let me pray for you:

O Lord God! I beseech thee, and through personal prayer intercession today that the Holy Spirit will touch this precious soul reading this book and turn their life around. Spirit of God, possess this loved one. Lord, overcome all dominating, controlling forces that have prevailed over their lives. I come against all oppressive thought, in Jesus Name. Henceforth; I pronounce you free—from manipulation, intimidation and domination of the wicked enemy called the devil. You are free from all satanic harassment and assaults. Amen.

TIME TO WALK
IN THE REALITY OF NEW BIRTH

Although the reason you became a Born Again Christian is so that you will enjoy eternity with Christ, while you are in this physical world you must walk in the reality of new birth.

Above all contradictions, you must prosper financially—as this is one of the wonders of new birth. You must understand and comprehend the scope of the things of the Spirit. Faith is a primary evidence of walking in the reality of new birth.

You must walk in Faith and not in fear of all things.

ABOUT THE AUTHOR

Rev. Franklin N. Abazie is the founding and Presiding Pastor of Miracle of God Ministries, with headquarters in Newark, New Jersey USA and a branch church in Owerri-Imo State Nigeria. He is following the footsteps of one of his mentors, the healing evangelist Oral Roberts of the blessed memory. The Lord passed Oral Roberts' healing mantle two days before he went to be with the Lord at age 91 into the hands of healing evangelist Rev. Franklin N. Abazie in a vision.

In all his services, the Power and Presence of God is present to heal all in his audience. Rev. Abazie is an ordained man of God, with a Healing Ministry reviving the healing and miracle ministry of Jesus Christ of Nazareth.

Pastor Franklin N. Abazie, has been called by God with a unique mandate: **"THE MOMENT IS DUE TO IMPACT YOUR WORLD THROUGH THE REVIVAL OF THE HEALING AND MIRACLE MINISTRY OF JESUS CHRIST OF NAZARETH.**

"I AM SENDING YOU TO RESTORE HEALTH UNTO THEE AND I WILL HEAL THEE OF THY WOUNDS, SAID THE LORD OF HOST."

Rev. Abazie is a gifted, ardent teacher of the word of God, who operates also in the office of a Prophet, generating and attracting undeniable signs and wonders, special miracles and healings, with apostolic fireworks of the Holy Ghost. He is the founding and presiding senior Pastor of this fast growing Healing Ministry. He has written over 86 inspirational, healing and transforming books covering almost all aspects of divine healing and life. He is happily married and blessed with children.

BOOKS BY REV. FRANKLIN N. ABAZIE:

1) The Outcome of Faith
2) Understanding the Secret of Prevailing Prayers
3) Commanding Abundance
4) Understanding the Secret of the Man God Uses
5) Activating My Due Season
6) Overcoming Divine Verdicts
7) The Outcome of Divine Wisdom
8) Understanding God's Restoration Mandate
9) Walking In the Victory and Authority of the Truth
10) God's Covenant Exemption
11) Destiny Restoration Pillars
12) Provoking Acceptable Praise
13) Understanding Divine Judgment
14) Activating Angelic Re-enforcement
15) Provoking Un-Merited Favo
16) The Benefits of the Speaking Faith
17) Understanding Divine Arrangement
18) How to Keep Your Healing
19) Understanding the Mysteries of the Speaking Faith
20) Understanding the Mysteries of Prophetic Healing
21) Operating Under the Rules of Creative Healing
22) Understanding the Joy of Breakthrough
23) Understanding the Mystery of Breakthrough
24) Understanding Divine Prosperity
25) Understanding Divine Healing
26) Retaining Your Inheritance
27) Overcoming Confusing Spirit
28) Commanding Angelic Escorts

29) *Enforcing Your Inheritance In Christ Jesus*
30) *Understanding Your Guardian Angels*
31) *Overcoming the Dominion of Sin*
32) *Understanding the Voice of God*
33) *The Outstanding Benefits of the Anointing*
34) *The Audacity of the Blood of Jesus*
35) *Walking in the Reality of the Anointing*
36) *Escaping the Nightmare of Poverty*
37) *Understanding Your Harvest Season*
38) *Activating Your Success Buttons*
39) *Overcoming the Forces of Darkness*
40) *Overcoming the Devices of the Devil*
41) *Overcoming Demonic Agents*
42) *Overcoming the Sorrows of Failure*
43) *Rejecting the Sorrows of Failure*
44) *Resisting the Sorrows of Poverty*
45) *Restoring Broken Marriages*
46) *Redeeming Your Days*
47) *The Force of Vision*
48) *Overcoming the Forces of Ignorance*
49) *Understanding the Sacrifice of Small Beginning*
50) *The Might of Small Beginning*
51) *Understanding the Mysteries of Prophesy*
52) *Overcoming Dream Nightmares*
53) *Breaking the Shackles of the Curse of the Law*
54) *Understanding the Joy of Harvest*
55) *Wisdom for Signs & Wonders*
56) *Wisdom for Generational Impact*
57) *Wisdom for Marriage Stability*
58) *Understanding the Number of Your Days*

59) *Enforcing Your Kingdom Rights*
60) *Escaping the Traps of Immoralities*
61) *Escaping the Trap of Poverty*
62) *Accessing Biblical Prosperity*
63) *Accessing True Riches in Christ*
64) *Silencing the Voice of the Accuser*
65) *Overcoming the Forces of Oppositions*
66) *Quenching the Voice of the Avenger*
67) *Silencing Demonic Prediction & Projection*
68) *Silencing Your Mocker*
69) *Understanding the Power of the Holy Ghost*
70) *Understanding the Baptism of Power*
71) *The Mystery of the Blood of Jesus*
72) *Understanding the Mystery of Sanctification*
73) *Understanding the Power of Holiness*
74) *Understanding the Forces of Purity & Righteousness*
75) *Activating the Forces of Vengeance*
76) *Appreciating the Mystery of Restoration*
77) *Overcoming the Projection & Prediction of the Enemy*
78) *Engaging the Mystery of the Blood*
79) *Commanding the Power of the Speaking Faith*
80) *Uprooting the Forces Against Your Rising*
81) *Overcoming Mere Success Syndrome*
82) *Understanding Divine Sentence*
83) *Understanding the Mystery of Praise*
84) *Understanding the Author of Faith*
85) *The Mystery of the Finisher of Faith*
86) *Attracting Supernatural Favor*

MIRACLE OF GOD MINISTRIES

NIGERIA CRUSADE 2012

MIRACLE OF GOD MINISTRIES
NIGERIA CRUSADE
2012

MIRACLE OF GOD MINISTRIES
NIGERIA CRUSADE 2012

MIRACLE OF GOD MINISTRIES

NIGERIA CRUSADE

2012

MIRACLE OF GOD MINISTRIES

NIGERIA CRUSADE

2012

www.ingramcontent.com/pod-product-compliance
Lightning Source LLC
Chambersburg PA
CBHW021449080526
44588CB00009B/767